FOUNDATIONS

Structure and Function of Government

COLIN
BAIN

SUSAN
ALIPHAT

DENNIS
DESRIVIERES

GRAHAM
JARVIS

ANGUS
SCULLY

CONTENTS

Prentice Hall Ginn Canada
Scarborough, Ontario

THE STRUCTURE OF GOVERNMENT

Time Line of a General Election

Prime minister asks governor general to call a general election. Chief elections officer issues documents to authorize holding an election in all ridings across Canada.	**Day 1**
Interested people have until this point to file their papers stating that they will be candidates in the election.	**Day 19**
Advance polls are held, allowing voters who will be away from home on election day to vote. (Results are not announced at this point.)	**Days 37-41**
An election is held in each riding.	**Day 47**
The prime minister and cabinet are sworn in by the governor general.	**Day 57 (approx.)**
The new House of Commons meets for the first time. The next election must be called (though not necessarily held) within five years of this date.	**Day 110 (approx.)**

What Do Politicians Say?

Speaker: Ovide Mercredi   **Date/Place:** 12 June 1991; Winnipeg, Manitoba
Occasion: He had just won the leadership of the Assembly of First Nations

I want the Minister [of Indian Affairs and Northern Development] to know that at the age of three months I was already being conditioned to be some tough nut.... But I want also to remind [all Canadians] that we will approach them in the way our ancestors approached them — with generosity.

Speaker: Kim Campbell   **Date/Place:** 13 June 1993; Calgary, Alberta
Occasion: She had just won the leadership of the Progressive Conservative party, and become Canada's 19th prime minister

You have honoured me by your trust and I return it with my complete commitment to live up to your trust. I invite each and every one of you to join with us for the greater battle that lies ahead and the real prize — a third majority government. Our party will always need people like you.

Speaker: Jean Chretien   **Date/Place:** 26 October 1993; Shawinigan, Quebec
Occasion: He had just led the Liberal party to victory in a general election, to become Canada's 20th prime minister

I will always appeal to the best in every citizen in our land. I will try to bring us together by appealing not to what divides us, but what unites us. We have, together, to realize the hopes and dreams of Canadians. We have a lot of work to do....

We have to concentrate all our efforts on the economy to create jobs. Together we will work hard and Canada will enter the twenty-first century as a proud, united, independent, generous nation....

I accept with humility the chance to prepare Canadians for the twenty-first century.

- Identify any topics or themes common to these speeches.

- Choose four adjectives that describe the mood of the speakers (e.g., modest, optimistic).

- Imagine that you have just been elected leader of your school's student government. Write a three-paragraph victory speech to be given to the whole school at an assembly. Try to model in your speech (a) the themes and (b) the adjectives you identified above.

- Compare your speech with that of a classmate. Which speech makes most effective use of the themes and adjectives you have identified? What makes the speech most effective?

- Listen to a politician speaking on radio or television. In what ways is the speech similar to or different from the extracts above?

FIGURE 1–1
Some of the candidates for the leadership of the Assembly of First Nations speak at an all-candidates meeting. What is the purpose of such meetings?

FIGURE 1–2
Pre-election campaigning: Jean Chretien meets members of the public. What is the purpose of this sort of activity?

Looking Forward

- What is a federal system of government?

- What do Canada's major political parties believe?

- How do Canadians vote, and what powers do voters have?

- How representative is parliament of Canada's diverse population?

Key Words

- federal system of government
- members of parliament (MPs)
- representation by population
- municipality
- bylaws
- political parties
- candidates
- riding
- ballot

3

How Our National and Provincial Governments Work

Canada's government system is a **federal** one. This means that we have two levels of government — one national government in Ottawa, and ten provincial governments. In addition, Yukon and the Northwest Territories have their own governments, supervised by the national government. Voters choose representatives to go to Ottawa, or their provincial or territorial capital, to represent their concerns.

In the national government, our representatives sit in the House of Commons, located in Ottawa. Representatives — or **members of parliament (MPs)** — come from each region of the country. The greater the number of people who live in a province or territory, the more members of parliament that province or territory has in Ottawa. This principle is known as **representation by population**.

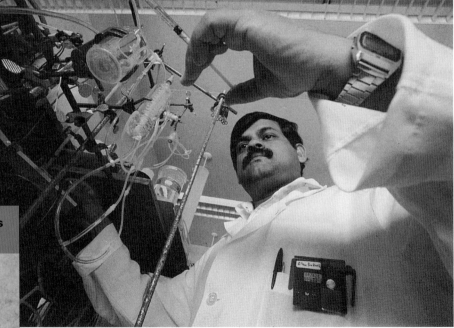

The national government in Ottawa makes laws dealing with such things as:

• national defence

• international trade

• Aboriginal affairs

• the banking system

• coins and banknotes

• marriage and divorce

• criminal law

FIGURE 1–3

Why do you think the federal government has responsibility for banking?

Provincial governments make laws about such things as :

• education

• health

• hospitals and charities

• local governments

• operation of the court system

FIGURE 1–4

Why do you think it is the provincial government's responsibility to make laws about services such as health?

CANADA
Population: 29 248 100
MPs: 295

FIGURE 1–5

Population and number of MPs from each region of Canada, 1994. In 1995, parliament agreed in principle to add 6 new members to the House of Commons because of population growth. In the first national election after 1995, Ontario's members would increase from 99 to 103, and British Columbia's from 32 to 34.

Table 1–1 Number of representatives in legislature of each province

Province	Members of legislature
Newfoundland and Labrador	52
Nova Scotia	52
Prince Edward Island	32
New Brunswick	58
Quebec	125
Ontario	130
Manitoba	57
Saskatchewan	66
Alberta	83
British Columbia	75

Table 1–2 Who governs?

National government	Provincial government
Crown (Queen or King)	Crown (Queen or King)
Governor general (Representative of the Crown in Canada)	Lieutenant governor (Representative of the Crown in the province)
Prime minister (Leader of political party with the most seats)	Premier (Leader of political party with the most seats)
Members of Parliament (MPs)	Members of Provincial Parliament (MPPs) or Members of Legislative Assembly (MLAs) or in Quebec only, Members of the National Assembly

Government and Taxes

Both the national and provincial levels of government can place taxes on the people. By raising money through taxes, our governments are able to pay for the services they provide, such as schools, hospitals, and the Canadian Armed Forces.

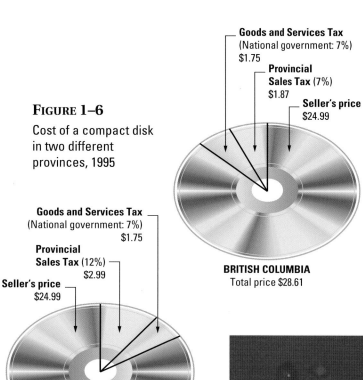

FIGURE 1–6

Cost of a compact disk in two different provinces, 1995

Goods and Services Tax (National government: 7%) $1.75

Provincial Sales Tax (7%) $1.87

Seller's price $24.99

BRITISH COLUMBIA
Total price $28.61

Goods and Services Tax (National government: 7%) $1.75

Provincial Sales Tax (12%) $2.99

Seller's price $24.99

NEWFOUNDLAND AND LABRADOR
Total price $29.73

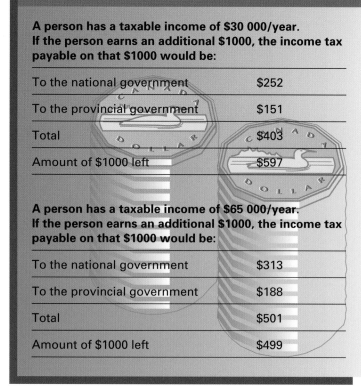

Table 1–3 Amount of income tax payable in Ontario, 1995

A person has a taxable income of $30 000/year. If the person earns an additional $1000, the income tax payable on that $1000 would be:

To the national government	$252
To the provincial government	$151
Total	$403
Amount of $1000 left	$597

A person has a taxable income of $65 000/year. If the person earns an additional $1000, the income tax payable on that $1000 would be:

To the national government	$313
To the provincial government	$188
Total	$501
Amount of $1000 left	$499

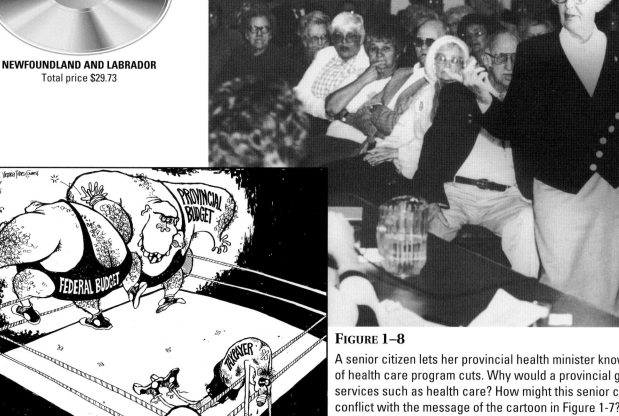

FIGURE 1–8

A senior citizen lets her provincial health minister know what she thinks of health care program cuts. Why would a provincial government cut services such as health care? How might this senior citizen's view conflict with the message of the cartoon in Figure 1-7?

FIGURE 1–7

What is this cartoon's message about taxes?

Activities

1. Which province has the highest population? Which province has the highest number of representatives in the House of Commons? Which province has the lowest population? Which province has the lowest number of representatives in the House of Commons? What general principle do you notice?

2. What are four things about which the national government makes laws? What are four things about which the provincial governments make laws?

3. Name three different taxes that our governments place on us to pay for government programs.

4. Look at Table 1–1. It lists the number of representatives that each province has in its legislature. Compare these figures with the population figures in Figure 1–5. Divide each of the provincial populations by the number of members in its legislature. (For example, Newfoundland and Labrador: 571 000÷52 = 10 980.8.) To what extent is the population of each province and the number of representatives related? Explain, using figures from the table and map.

5. a) Using the *Canada Yearbook* or an almanac with information about Canada, find out how much of the national government's current revenue comes from the areas listed in the organizer below. Make an organizer similar to this one to record your information.

   b) Income taxes tend to fall more heavily on richer people. The more you earn, the higher the percentage you pay in tax. The GST tends to fall more heavily on lower income people, who have to spend a larger percentage of their income on daily living expenses. Prepare a one-page speech, in which you argue for or against changing the balance between income tax and GST revenues.

Item	Amount ($ billions)	% of total
Personal income taxes		
Corporate income taxes		
Goods and Services Tax (GST)		
Canada Pension contributions		
Unemployment Insurance contributions		
Alcohol taxes		
Tobacco taxes		
Fuel taxes		
Customs duties		
Fees and licences		
Other income		
Total		**100.0**

How Our Local Governments Work

In addition to the national and provincial governments, there is a third level. This is known as local government. This level deals with providing services for a city, town, or county. Where a local government has responsibility for a city, it is called a **municipal** government. (A city area controlled by a local government is called a **municipality**.) Local governments pass **bylaws**, or regulations, that apply only in that area.

The operation of municipal governments varies among the provinces. In Alberta, for example, elections take place in October, while in Ontario they take place in November. Similarly, the titles of the elected members vary. Figure 1–9 illustrates the structure of a typical municipal government.

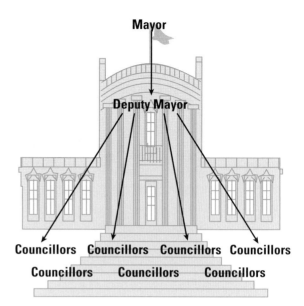

FIGURE 1–9
Typical municipal government structure

Local governments make bylaws about such things as:

- providing garbage collection and disposal services

- providing fire protection services

- zoning land for industrial, commercial, agricultural, or residential purposes

- issuing building permits and ensuring that land is used according to the zoning regulations

- providing police services (generally in larger municipalities only)

- setting limits on store opening and closing hours

- collecting annual property taxes and fees for many licences — for example, pet licences or store licences — to pay for the services provided

FIGURE 1–10
The mayor is the chief official of a municipality. Top: Mayor Léopold Belliveau of Moncton, New Brunswick, in ceremonial dress. Left: Mayor Shirley Kalyniuk of Rossburn, Manitoba, accepts a cheque from a provincial politician that will help pay for improved transit services in the municipality.

- In Toronto, home owners must clear the sidewalks in front of their homes within 12 hours of a snowfall.

- In Vancouver, pet owners must clean up after their dogs when in any public area.

- In London, Ontario, residents must not make loud noise after 23:00 — by playing stereos, radios, etc., or through noisy or boisterous behaviour.

- In Calgary, cats must not stray beyond their owner's property. A violation costs the owner $100.

- In Halifax, Nova Scotia, residents may not place garbage cans in the street before the scheduled day of collection.

- In many municipalities, smoking in restaurants is permitted only in designated areas.

DOES YOUR DOG HAVE A LICENSE?

All dogs 3 months and older must be licensed.
Apply now . . . it's as easy as picking up the phone
and calling 268-4350.
Bylaw officers will be going door to door
to ensure that your dog is licensed.
The penalty for an unlicensed dog
is now $250.00.
Be a responsible pet owner.

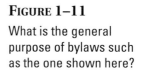

 THE CITY
OF CALGARY

Animal Services Section
3990 Manchester Rd. S.E.

FIGURE 1–11

What is the general purpose of bylaws such as the one shown here?

FIGURE 1–12

"Municipal government is all about communities. It is where resident groups, community organizations, and local businesses bring their immediate concerns and issues. Local government works well when it encourages the active involvement of all the players in the community."— Olivia Chow, Councillor for Toronto Downtown, Municipality of Metropolitan Toronto

6. a) Name four different services about which local governments may make bylaws.

b) In what different ways do local governments raise money to pay for the services they provide?

7. Make an organizer similar to the one below. Do some research and complete the organizer to show the situation where you live. Follow the example.

Government Responsibilities in My Part of Canada

Item	Level responsible	Details
Penalty for first degree murder	Federal government	Life imprisonment. (Minimum 25 years)
Age at which you must begin school		
Name/location of nearest Armed Forces base		
Cost of a permit to build a single-family home		
How often (if at all) garbage is collected		
Name/location of nearest First Nations friendship centre		
Tuition fees for one year of college or university		
Cost of a dog licence		
Name/location of nearest bank		
Name/location of nearest hospital		
Name/location of nearest food bank		
Name/location of nearest family crisis centre		
Where you would go to find the nearest legal aid lawyer		

8. a) Do some research to find out about some of the bylaws in effect where you live. Make a list of five bylaws, and fill in an organizer similar to the one below. Follow the example.

b) Imagine that you have been asked to write a letter to the editor of your local newspaper, in favour of or opposed to one of the bylaws. Write the letter, clearly stating your position, your reasons for it, and actions people should take to convince their local councillors that your position is correct.

What the bylaw says	Groups that might favour the bylaw	Groups that might oppose the bylaw
Gas stations may not open on Sunday	• Practising Christians	• Members of other religious groups
		• Labour unions
		• Business groups

How Canadians Vote

In choosing people to represent them in parliament, voters frequently look at **political parties**. Parties are groups of people with similar beliefs about how the country should be run. They put forward **candidates**, or people trying to be elected, in many different areas of the country.

Voters choose only one of the candidates for their own **riding**. A riding is any area that can choose a candidate as its representative in government. There are 295 ridings represented in Canada's national government.

FIGURE 1–13

Candidates and their parties work hard to attract votes. What different methods are shown here? What type of audience does each piece aim to attract? Which do you find the most effective? Explain.

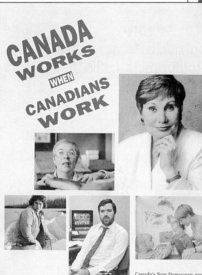

CANADA WORKS WHEN CANADIANS WORK

Canada's New Democrats present

A Strategy for Full Employment

mission des peuples autochtones
riginal Peoples' Commission

Liberal Party of Canada
Parti libéral du Canada

BELIEVING in the right of all Aboriginal people to participate in the political process in Canada in order to achieve a just and equitable position for Aboriginal peoples in Canadian society;
COMMITTED to the socio-economic betterment of Aboriginal people, and the recognition of the Aboriginal and treaty rights of Aboriginal peoples, including the inherent right of self-determination;
DEDICATED to the creation of a caring society and healthy environment in which all peoples may peacefully flourish in harmony with our Mother the Earth, so as to ensure a place for our generations to come;
BELIEVING that the philosophy and ideology of the Liberal Party of Canada is compatible with the aspirations of Aboriginal people and best suited to accommodate the interests of Aboriginal people in Canada; and
THEREFORE the Aboriginal Peoples' Commission is constituted as a commission of the Liberal Party of Canada with the principle objectives of representing and promoting the interests of Aboriginal peoples within the Liberal Party of Canada and encouraging the active participation of Aboriginal people at all levels within the Party.

200 ouest, avenue Laurier Avenue West, Ottawa, Ontario - KIP 6M8 - Tel: (613) 237-0740 - Fax: (613) 235-7208

Preston **MANNING**

REFORM

KILLS BUGS | KILLS MICE | KILLS JOBS

ONTARIANS FOR RESPONSIBLE GOVERNMENT (416) 869-3838

FIGURE 1–14

"Dirty advertising": After the New Democratic Party won a provincial election in Ontario with a large majority in 1991, a group opposed to the NDP mounted a campaign to sway the opinion of the public with billboards such as the one shown here. The man shown is Bob Rae who, as leader of Ontario's NDP, was premier of the province from 1991 to 1995. What do you think of this kind of advertising? Is it effective? Is it fair?

Table 1–4
In the 1993 national election, five political parties had candidates elected to the House of Commons. This table shows what they said about some of the key issues. Do a media survey over the course of the next month. Which of these issues still appear to be important to your politicians? What additional issues appear to be important now?

Political party	Jobs	Cutting government costs	Social programs
Liberals	Start a two-year program, costing $6 billion, to create 10 000 jobs.	Moderate cuts, but not to social programs.	Maintain and slightly increase government spending on health and education.
Progressive Conservatives	Jobs should be created by business, not by government. Government should support businesses in creating jobs.	$8 billion in cuts every year until 1997.	Maintain adequate spending; figures not given.
New Democrats	Abolish GST. Start a $40 billion fund for new businesses to create 500 000 jobs.	Cut $2.2 billion each year for five years.	Create 300 000 new day-care spaces; spend $100 million on new houses. New taxes on businesses and the rich to pay for government programs.
Reform	Reduce immigration by 50 percent, until economy improves.	Cut $6.3 billion each year for three years. Raise $5.5 billion in new taxes each year.	Keep most valuable programs (e.g., health services). Cut others (e.g., pensions for the rich).
Bloc Quebecois	Spend $5 billion to create new jobs.	Cut $3.3 billion each year for three years.	Keep payments to provinces (for services such as health and education) at present levels. Put half into job creation. Reduce taxes for families.

A Federal Election in One Riding

Winnipeg North is, as its name suggests, a riding in the northern part of Manitoba's capital city. About 65 000 voters live in the riding. In the 1993 election, eight candidates tried to become MP for the riding.

When voters record their choice, they are given a **ballot** — the official voting paper (see Figure 1–16). Voters must choose only one candidate from the list. They do this by placing an "X" in the circle beside the candidate they prefer. If a voter chooses more than one candidate, or numbers the candidates in order of preference, the ballot is not counted.

When voting finished in Winnipeg North, the ballots were counted. The result is shown in Table 1–5. Rey Pagtakhan was declared the winner, because he had more votes than anyone else. He received 22 180 votes out of 43 299 (or about 51 percent of total votes cast). Candidates do not need to win a majority of votes in their riding, only to get more votes than anyone else. Even if Mr. Pagtakhan had received 5000 votes fewer than he did, he would still have gone to Ottawa as the riding's representative.

FIGURE 1–15

Stages in an election

Before an election, enumerators go door to door in each riding, to register eligible voters.

At the polling station, scrutineers check that each voter is eligible and, later, count ballots.

FIGURE 1–16

The ballot for the federal election in Winnipeg North, 1993, looked like this.

Each voter marks an "X" beside the candidate he or she prefers.

Voters fold their ballots and slip them through the slot in a closed box.

Results are tabulated as the ballots in each box are counted. Computerized tabulation is becoming increasingly common.

Table 1–5 Results in Winnipeg North, 1993

Candidate	Votes
Lynn Filbert	1 992
Joe Lynch	135
Rey Pagtakhan	22 180
Frederico Papetti	211
Anna Polonyi	767
Mary Stanley	184
Judy Wasylycia-Leis	13 706
Mike Wiens	4 124

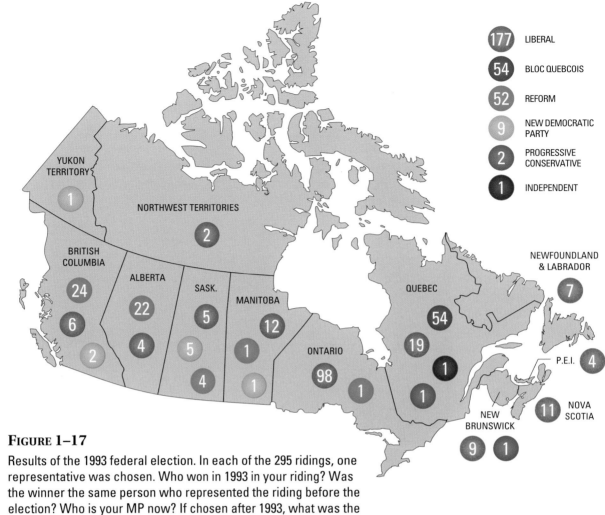

FIGURE 1–17

Results of the 1993 federal election. In each of the 295 ridings, one representative was chosen. Who won in 1993 in your riding? Was the winner the same person who represented the riding before the election? Who is your MP now? If chosen after 1993, what was the reason (a by-election, a new general election, etc.)?

Legend:
- 177 LIBERAL
- 54 BLOC QUEBCOIS
- 52 REFORM
- 9 NEW DEMOCRATIC PARTY
- 2 PROGRESSIVE CONSERVATIVE
- 1 INDEPENDENT

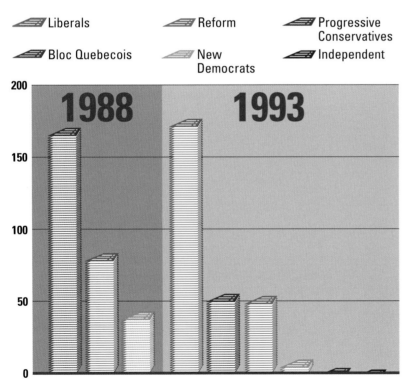

Legend: Liberals, Reform, Progressive Conservatives, Bloc Quebecois, New Democrats, Independent

FIGURE 1–18

Number of elected MPs in Canada, by party, 1988 and 1993

In an election, the party that wins the most seats becomes the government. The leader of the winning party becomes the prime minister, but this person must also be chosen as the representative of one of the ridings. While all American voters have an opportunity to vote for their president, in Canada only the voters in an individual riding can vote directly for the person who becomes prime minister.

Elections can have a great impact on the people who represent us. This was shown more clearly than ever before in the election of 1993. Consider the results shown in Figure 1–18. Who won the election of 1988? What happened to this party in 1993? Which two parties were new in 1993? How did they do in the election? These results came as a surprise to many Canadians. Why do you think this was so?

FIGURE 1–19

The Bloc Quebecois, under the leadership of Lucien Bouchard (right), and the Reform Party, under Preston Manning, won over 100 seats combined in 1993, although both were relatively new parties. Check Figure 1–17 to see which parts of the country supported these two parties.

FIGURE 1–20

Kim Campbell, Progressive Conservative member of parliament for the riding of Vancouver Centre, lost her seat in 1993, even though she was prime minister at the time of the election.

FIGURE 1–21

Svend Robinson, MP for Burnaby-Kingsway, was the only New Democrat from Vancouver to keep his seat in the 1993 election.

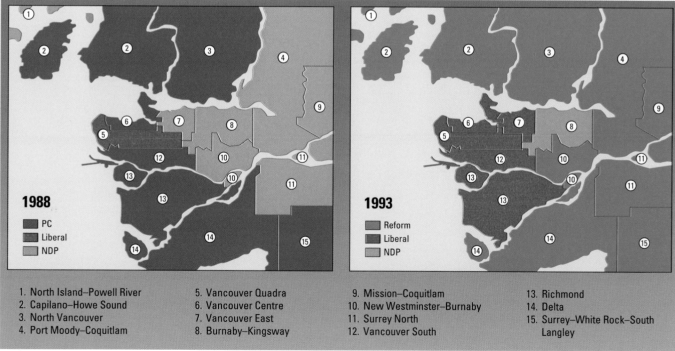

1988
- PC
- Liberal
- NDP

1993
- Reform
- Liberal
- NDP

1. North Island–Powell River
2. Capilano–Howe Sound
3. North Vancouver
4. Port Moody–Coquitlam
5. Vancouver Quadra
6. Vancouver Centre
7. Vancouver East
8. Burnaby–Kingsway
9. Mission–Coquitlam
10. New Westminster–Burnaby
11. Surrey North
12. Vancouver South
13. Richmond
14. Delta
15. Surrey–White Rock–South Langley

FIGURE 1–22

How Vancouver voted, 1988 and 1993. Which two parties held the most seats in Vancouver after the 1988 election? How did results differ in 1993? What do these results say about the power of voters?

9. What is the major difference between the American way of choosing a president and the Canadian way of choosing a prime minister?

10. a) Look over the positions of the five political parties in Table 1–4. Which issues seem to have been important to many of the parties? Which issues seem to have been important to only a few of the parties?
   b) If you had been a voter, which issue do you think would have been the most important to you? Explain.
   c) The caption for Table 1–4 asks you to do a media survey to identify key issues of concern to political parties today. Prepare a display of your findings.

11. a) In the 1993 election, 71 percent of all eligible voters actually voted. If Winnipeg North contained 65 000 eligible voters, what percentage actually voted there? Was it higher or lower than the national figure?
   b) What percentage of the votes cast went to each candidate in Winnipeg North?
   c) Was Rey Pagtakhan's victory a comfortable one? Explain, using figures.

12. Look at the map in Figure 1–17. Which party seems to have gained support in all regions of the country? Which parties seem to have gained support in only one or more regions? Use figures from the map to support your conclusions.

13. Look at the maps in Figure 1–22. How many seats were gained or lost by each of the following as a result of the 1993 election?
   a) Progressive Conservatives
   b) Liberals
   c) New Democrats
   d) Reform
   What conclusions can you draw?

14. From the evidence in Figures 1–17 and 1–22, would you say that voting patterns are similar or different across the country? Use figures and name different regions to explain your answer.

15. A party's leader is very important to its appeal to the voters. Choose the leader of one political party (either national or provincial/territorial).
   a) Research the following topics.
      i) How long was this person in politics before becoming party leader?
      ii) What qualities enabled the person to become party leader?

   iii) How successful has the leader been in appealing to voters?
   iv) What changes has the leader made to the party's position on any key issues?
   v) Do you consider the leader to be a good politician? Explain.
   b) Prepare a visual display, with pictures and explanations, to summarize your findings.

16. Research political representation in Canada today. Which of the following items have changed since the 1993 election? Complete an organizer similar to the one below.

In 1993	True/false today	Explanation
The Liberal party became the government.		
Jean Chretien became prime minister.		
The Bloc Quebecois became the official opposition.		
Lucien Bouchard became leader of the opposition.		
The Reform Party won many seats in western Canada		
The New Democratic Party won very few seats.		
The Progressive Conservative Party was almost wiped out in parliament.		

17. a) With a partner, do some research into recent national election campaigns. In addition, research the last election campaign in your province or territory.
   b) One partner should play the role of TV interviewer, and the other an expert on election campaigns. Write the script for a short TV interview in which the interviewer tries to find out whether there is any truth to the statement, "It is the mistakes of the losers, not the actions of the winners, that result in election victories."

Reflecting Diversity:
The Changing Face of Parliament

54 women will be going to Parliament

Women made a historic breakthrough in the federal election, winning substantially more seats than in any previous elections.

Fifty-four women will be going to Parliament, 16 more than were elected in 1988. This represents slightly less than 20 percent of the 295 seats in the House of Commons….

So will the presence of all these women change the way business is done in the Commons? Is the noisy…old boys' club a thing of the past?

Rookie member Jean Augustine from Etobicoke-Lakeshore in Toronto said a number of celebrated incidents in Parliament…have served to "clear the dinosaurs out of the woodwork."

She acknowledged that Liberal women will run the risk of being considered annoying lobbyists within their own party if they repeatedly push women's issues. "But it is the risk one takes to move things forward."…

"There is something in our approach to problem solving," Shaughnessy Cohen, newly elected member from Windsor, Ontario, said. "Women are raised…to be problem solvers. If the House of Commons is an old boys' club, it will change because of our presence."

FIGURE 1–23

Three women elected in 1993: (top) Sheila Finestone, Secretary of State for Multiculturalism, discusses ways to promote racial and cultural diversity in the work force, with the Head of the Conference Board of Canada; (left) Jean Augustine congratulates new Canadians at a citizenship ceremony; (above right) Ethel Blondin-Andrew, who was first elected in 1988. She was the first woman representative from a First Nation to sit in the House of Commons.

FIGURE 1–24

"I'm proud to be a Sikh, but first of all a Canadian." — Gurbax Malhi, elected in Bramalea-Gore-Malton, Ontario, in 1993

FIGURE 1–25

"In my capacity as Secretary of State for Asia-Pacific, I travel overseas to increase relations between Canada and the countries of the Asia-Pacific region. I see myself as a bridge, not only while I am outside of Canada, but also while I am at home." —Raymond Chan, elected in Richmond, British Columbia, in 1993

Minorities in a Majority Government

HOWEVER you cut it, it was the "community vote" that clinched the Liberal victory....

Now there are some competent MPs who could begin to change things, some of whom have spent many years fighting for the rights of minorities.

• One of Jean Chretien's senior ministers is likely to be Sergio Marchi who has high recognition among Italian Canadians and other minorities....

• Sheila Finestone from Mount Royal, in Montreal, has done well in the cultural community as well as in the Canadian Jewish community.

• And don't pass by Rey Pagtakhan from Winnipeg who has headed the Filipino Canadian national organization....

Source: Adapted from A. Cardoz, Toronto Star, November 2, 1993, p. A20.

A Vote for Change

WE SUPPORTED Jean Chretien because he provided us with the best available candidates — regardless of gender, ethnicity, country of origin, or religion.

Prior to the election, Chretien and his team demonstrated the party's new vision by seriously seeking out candidates who could not only win their ridings but who also have the potential to successfully help run this country and make it prosperous.

It is significant to note that when the Liberals take their seats in the House of Commons in Ottawa, the makeup will be more reflective of Canada as it is today.

Included in the 177 Liberal members of parliament are three who are originally from the Caribbean, two Sikhs, a Filipino, a Chinese, a South Asian, and three Native Canadians.

Source: Adapted from Share, October 28, 1993, p. 8.

Activities

18. How many seats are there in the House of Commons? How many were occupied by women as a result of the 1993 election? What was the most important benefit the women MPs hoped they could bring to Parliament?

19. Why is it important that an equitable (fair) number of MPs should be female, people of colour, and representatives of cultural communities? What benefits do you think such MPs can bring to Canada's political system?

20. a) Find out how many elected members there are in your local government. Find out how many of these people are:

   i)   female
   ii) people of colour
   iii) members of First Nations
   iv) disabled

   b) Find out how each of the above groups is represented in the general population of your community.
   c) Make a bar graph to show the following:
      i)   the percentage of each group in the general community
      ii) the percentage of each group in your local government
   d) What conclusions can you draw about how representative your local government is?

PUTTING IT TOGETHER

1 This chapter has shown the diversity of the Canadian political process.

> **diversity** having differences, variety

For each of the following, write a paragraph that shows how diversity exists in Canadian political life. Support your answers with figures taken from this chapter or from your own research of the current federal government. To help you get started, one example has been done for you.

a) The number of seats each province or territory has in the House of Commons.

There is great diversity in the numbers of seats that the provinces and territories have in the House of Commons. Prince Edward Island, the smallest province, has four members in the House. Ontario, the largest, has 99. So Ontario has almost 25 times as many members as P.E.I. Yukon and Northwest Territories have even fewer members than the smallest province. We can say that there is great diversity, with numbers of members ranging from very few up to a large number.

b) The way provinces vote in federal elections.

c) The regions of the country from which the federal cabinet comes.
d) The various backgrounds from which MPs come.
e) The number of votes won by the various parties in a particular riding.
f) The ideas of the different political parties on how to create more jobs in Canada.

2 In this chapter, you have learned much about the various levels of government in Canada. Make an organizer similar to the one below, and complete it with information from this chapter. Follow the example.

Key terms relating to Canada's government		
Term	**Meaning**	**Purpose**
Cabinet	Prime minister and advisors chosen from MPs	Suggest bills to parliament that may become laws
Federal system		
MP		
Political party		
Candidate		
Riding		
Ballot		

PART 2

THE FUNCTIONS OF GOVERNMENT

An Interview with Rey Pagtakhan, MP for Winnipeg North

What did you do before you became an MP?

I was a pediatrician and professor of Pediatrics and Child Health at the University of Manitoba. I spent much of my professional life studying lung diseases in children.

Why did you decide to become an MP?

I grew up in the Philippines, and my family had very little money. I vowed early on that I would overcome my poverty, with education as the key. Then I would help others do the same. Canada, my adopted country since 1968, has given me many wonderful opportunities. Public service is a way to give something back.

What are the challenges of your job?

An MP's work is very time-consuming. The days are long and filled with meetings, speeches, correspondence, briefings, public appearances, media queries, and work for individual constituents. An MP has to be able to set priorities, to know the needs of constituents, and to find time for family and friends, as well.

What are the rewards of your job?

There is a tremendous sense of satisfaction in helping people deal with government offices and procedures. For many people, government is intimidating. Government is supposed to serve the people; my job is ensure that it does so. It is also very satisfying to participate in debate on national issues. And it is particularly rewarding to see some of your own suggestions become policy.

What advice would you give to a young person who is interested in eventually becoming an MP?

I would urge him or her to pursue that goal. Politics always needs fresh blood, young women and men concerned about the future of Canada and the world. Get involved where you live. Volunteer with local organizations whose mission is not necessarily political, but to provide services. Read about government and politics. Study history. And listen to people — never think you have all the answers. But don't prepare specifically for politics. First, pursue any career and try to excel.

Key Words

- bills
- cabinet
- ministers
- executive
- legislative
- judicial
- recall
- first past the post (FPTP)
- proportional representation (PR)
- FPTP-PR
- Triple-E Senate

FIGURE 2–1
Dr. Pagtakhan and Mrs. Pagtakhan with Prime Minister Chretien and Mrs. Chretien at a social function

FIGURE 2–2
Reform MP Jan Brown speaks to constituents.

FIGURE 2–3
NDP MP and former party leader Audrey McLaughlin speaks to the press.

FIGURE 2–4
Progressive Conservative MP and party leader Jean Charest speaks during a question and answer period at a national party convention.

Looking Forward

- What are the major responsibilities of an MP?

- What is the function of each part of government — executive, legislative, and judicial?

- What sorts of services does the federal government provide to its citizens?

- Does our system of government need reform, and, if so, in what areas?

The House of Commons at Work

The members of the House of Commons have two major responsibilities. First, they must represent the people in their ridings and try to help them with problems they might have. For example, a group of citizens might be trying to obtain funds to clean up a river and its valley, as it runs through a city. Their MP might be able to assist them in obtaining a grant for this purpose.

The second major responsibility of an MP is to take part in debates and to vote for or against new laws. The prime minister's party, the government, regularly introduces **bills** — that is, proposed laws — into the House. It is the job of the MPs to decide whether or not a bill should be passed. If a bill is passed in the House of Commons, it then goes to the other House of Parliament, the Senate. If it is also passed there, it will become a law.

The Cabinet

The prime minister asks some MPs to join the **cabinet**. This is the name given to the group that decides what the government's policy should be. The cabinet is made up of the prime minister and selected MPs who have special responsibilities. Members of parliament who are given cabinet responsibilities are known as **ministers**. By tradition, the prime minister chooses the cabinet from among his or her party's members of parliament.

Table 2–1 A typical cabinet would contain the following positions.

Position	Examples of responsibilities
Prime Minister	Choosing other cabinet members
Minister of Finance	Recommending tax and government spending policies
Minister of Revenue	Supervising collection and spending of government money
Minister for the Treasury Board	Payment of the government's employees and other bills
Minister of Government Services	Maintaining government buildings and property
Minister of Foreign Affairs	Supervising Canada's relations with other countries
Minister of Human Resources	Maintaining a skilled labour force; unemployment insurance
Minister of Immigration	Matters relating to immigrants, refugees, etc.
Minister of Defence	Canadian Armed Forces, overseas peacekeeping activities
Minister of the Environment	Maintaining clean and safe air, water, etc.
Minister of Natural Resources	Mines, minerals, etc.
Minister of Indian Affairs and Northern Development	Ensuring protection of the rights of First Nations
Minister of Justice	Drafting laws about criminal behaviour
Solicitor-General	Running the courts and legal system
Minister of Trade and Industry	Imports, exports, creation of jobs
Minister of Transport	Airlines, railroads, shipping
Minister of Fisheries and Oceans	Commercial fishing regulations

There are a number of other cabinet positions. In 1993, for example, the total membership was 24.

FIGURE 2–5

Cabinet ministers in action: (above) Environment Minister Sheila Copps helps clean up the harbour in Hamilton, Ontario, while some environmentalists protest that she is simply seeking publicity; (top right) Minister of Finance Paul Martin presents a budget in parliament, outlining the government's spending policies; (bottom right) Fisheries Minister Brian Tobin speaks to reporters, describing the size of fish found on a foreign ship stopped for fishing illegally off the Grand Banks.

Activities

1. What are the two major responsibilities of Canada's MPs?

2. a) What is the role of the cabinet?
   b) Who picks its members?
   c) By tradition, from which group of people is the cabinet picked?

3. Find out about the current cabinet.
   a) What is its total membership?
   b) What are the names of the people holding the positions indicated in Table 2–1, and which riding does each of them represent?
   c) How many members are women?
   d) How many members come from each province or territory?

4. Referring to your findings from question 3 and Part 1, if necessary, answer the following.
   a) Which areas of Canada appear to be properly represented in the cabinet? Which areas appear to be over-represented? Which areas appear to be under-represented?
   b) Are women and members of visible minorities properly represented in the present cabinet? Explain your answer.

5. Prepare a list of questions that you would like to put to a politician. Invite an elected politician into your school to find out the answers to your questions.

The Three Parts of Government

Imagine that a class of students is planning an all-day excursion to be taken at the end of the school year. The school allows only one day for recreational excursions, so the students have to make some choices about where they should go.

A small group is chosen to come up with suggestions. Members of the group review the possibilities before presenting the class with the following options.

> **Renata:** The first possibility is a trip to the city. We can spend the afternoon in the theme park, and go to a baseball game in the evening.
>
> **Fred:** The second option is to go out into the bush, a couple of hours from here, and spend the day learning about nature, orienteering skills, and canoeing.
>
> **Rashmi:** We estimate the total cost for each student for the city trip, including the bus, to be about $40. The cost of the bush trip would be about $10. So, if we all vote for the city trip, the group recommends that we hold a car wash to raise money towards the trip. We think $40 is too much for each student to pay. We think we can raise enough from the car wash to bring the cost for each student down to $15.

After much discussion, the whole class — including the small group — votes and, by 17 votes to 16, chooses the city trip. Soon a problem arises, however. The day of the car wash is very windy and wet, and the students have very few customers. As a result, students will have to pay $25 each towards the cost of the trip, much more than they had originally thought. At a class discussion, the following interchange takes place.

> **Bob:** Well, I think we should reconsider the original decision. Since it's going to cost us so much, after the car wash failure, we should think about taking the bush trip instead.
>
> **Benazir:** No. The majority voted for the city trip, so we should try to do it.
>
> **Ryan:** But if the class had known it would cost $25 to take the city trip, we probably wouldn't have voted for it.

After much discussion, but no agreement, the class decides to refer the dispute to the school principal. She works with the president of the student council to put together a proposal. The principal and president will lend the money from their school accounts to the class so that the cost of the city trip comes down to $15, as long as the class will agree to hold another car wash in September to pay the money back.

The students vote to accept the proposal. They all enjoy the trip. The money is repaid after a successful car wash in September.

FIGURE 2–6

In this scenario, a car wash is the form of raising revenue. How do governments raise revenue?

In this scenario, the class has done three things. First, a small group of students investigated the options and came up with two proposals. Second, a larger group (the whole class, including the small group), discussed the proposals and voted on what to do. Third, when a dispute arose among the students, a neutral group (the principal and the president) was called on to suggest a solution.

As Table 2–2 illustrates, this process is identical to the one used by governments. Our national and provincial governments are divided into three parts. The **executive** part, the cabinet, suggests possibilities for new laws to parliament. The **legislative** part, parliament, discusses and votes on possible new laws brought before it. The **judicial** part, the courts, referee between parties when there is a dispute about a law, and decide whether or not people have broken a law.

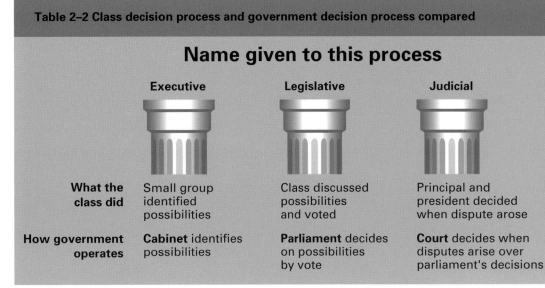

Table 2–2 Class decision process and government decision process compared

Name given to this process

	Executive	Legislative	Judicial
What the class did	Small group identified possibilities	Class discussed possibilities and voted	Principal and president decided when dispute arose
How government operates	**Cabinet** identifies possibilities	**Parliament** decides on possibilities by vote	**Court** decides when disputes arise over parliament's decisions

Activities

6. Complete an organizer similar to the one below, based on what you have read in this section.

Which part of government is at work?

Item	Part of government
a) The cabinet suggests raising income taxes.	Executive
b) Courts in Ontario must ensure that under-19s who buy tobacco products are tried fairly.	
c) Members of the House of Commons vote in favour of free trade with the US.	
d) Members of the Senate vote in favour of creating a new territory, to be known as Nunavut.	
e) The prime minister announces a new plan to increase the number of refugees allowed into Canada.	
f) Parliament votes to reduce payments to the provinces for welfare and post-secondary education.	
g) Cabinet considers a proposal to reduce the size of the Canadian Armed Forces.	
h) Courts begin to impose five-year prison terms (up from three-year terms) on young offenders convicted of first-degree murder, as the law now allows.	
i) The minister responsible signs a deal with First Nations in Manitoba giving them a greater degree of self-government.	
j) A court convicts a person of fare-dodging by placing worthless foreign coins in the fare box on a city bus.	

7. Look over back issues of a daily newspaper. Cut out six news stories relating to either the national government or a provincial government in Canada. For each story:
   a) Write a one-paragraph summary of the details.
   b) Identify which part of government — executive, legislative, or judicial — is being described in the news story, and explain how you know.

8. With a classmate, make up a collage of your news stories and written work.

Government Services to Citizens

Canadians expect much from their governments. As a result, governments have worked to supply a wide range of services. Canadians have come to expect everything from free education to grants of money to establish new industries. This display illustrates the wide variety of services offered by the federal government. Remember, however, that there are also provincial and local governments, providing different services.

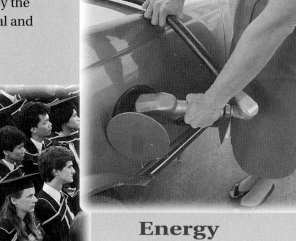

Energy

- Fuel consumption figures for new cars
- Investment in Hibernia oil/gas fields off Newfoundland
- Atomic Energy of Canada nuclear reactor sales abroad

Young people

- Support for universities
- Open House Canada (exchange program)
- Family allowance

Work

- Unemployment Insurance cheques
- Social Insurance numbers

Communications

- Supervising Canada Post Corporation
- Supporting Anik communications satellite
- Licensing radio and television stations

Well being

- Licensing banks
- Setting automobile safety standards
- Old Age Security payments

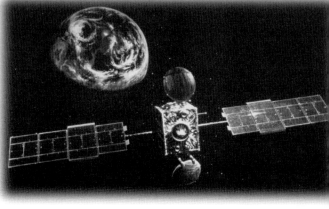

Economic development
- Collecting statistics
- Farm Support payments
- Fisheries support

Environment
- Automobile exhaust emissions regulations
- Environment Canada (weather forecasting)
- Fish and wildlife protection

Recreation
- National Parks
- Topographic maps
- Support for amateur athletes

Art and culture
- National Film Board
- National Archives (Ottawa)
- Museum of Civilization (Hull, Quebec)

Canadians abroad
- Issuing passports
- Customs and Immigration officers
- Canadian University Students Overseas (a volunteer foreign aid program)

Government in School and Society

There are many other governing bodies besides our national, provincial, and local governments. For example, does your school have a student government? Many schools have an organization, elected by the students, that aims to make school life more enjoyable for the students.

Student Government at Acton High School

Purpose/role: To organize social events, recreational activities, and charity events on behalf of the student body.

Structure: A four-person cabinet takes proposals to student council, where the proposals are debated and voted on. A teacher advisor assists the cabinet and council with proposals and carrying them out.

How members are chosen: Each student has two ballots. One is used to vote for members of cabinet. Candidates for the cabinet speak at assemblies to outline their plans, and the vote is held the next day. The second ballot is used to vote for grade representatives. Grade 10 students vote for Grade 10 candidates, Grade 11 for Grade 11 candidates, and so on. Candidates for grade representative speak at grade assemblies. Voting is held the next day, and each student may vote for four of the candidates. Each June, a new cabinet and council are chosen, and they take office the following September.

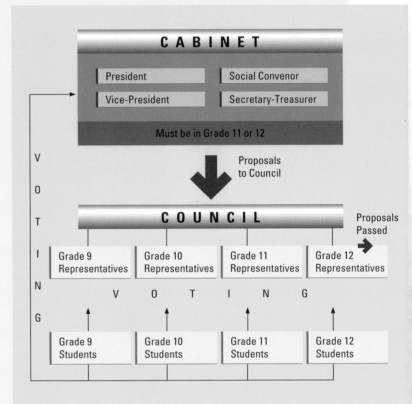

FIGURE 2–7

The structure of the student council at Acton High School

FIGURE 2–8

Members of a student council. What are the advantages of having a form of student government in a school?

Who is eligible to run for office: Any full-time student who has a satisfactory academic performance may run to be a grade representative. After a one-year term as a grade representative, a full-time student with a satisfactory academic performance may run for a cabinet position.

Value of student government: The members get experience in debating alternatives, making decisions, and organizing events. The student body has a voice in the life of the school.

9. From the display on pages 26 and 27, make a list of those federal government services you or your family use almost every day. Make a second list of those services you use at least once a month. Make a third list of those services you use at least once a year. How extensively does your family use these federal government services?

10. Do some research to find out the major services offered by provincial governments. Which five do you think are most commonly used? Why do you think so?

11. What is the purpose of the Acton High School student government? How does one become a member of it?

12. a) Find out about the structure of the student government in your school.
    b) Create a diagram of the student government at Acton High School and one of the student government at your school.
    c) Make notes to point out the similarities and differences between the two student governments.
    d) State which one you feel better represents the needs of the students, and why.

13. Imagine you were running for either grade representative or president of a student council.
    a) Find out some of the actions students would like the student council to take.
    b) Make a poster supporting your candidacy, designed to appeal to your fellow students.
    c) Write a short speech to the student body, explaining your qualifications, why you are seeking the position, and what you hope to do if elected.

14. Research the local government in your community. (It might be a city or town council, a rural council, or a regional council, depending on where you live.) Find out about its purpose/role, structure, and membership. Would you like to be a member of it in the future? Why or why not?

15. The national and provincial governments make grants to universities and colleges to help with their operations. In the early 1990s, government grants accounted for about 80 percent of university and college revenues. Students were paying only about 20 percent of the real cost of their education. Governments began to cut back on grants to post-secondary institutions, forcing them to raise tuition fees.
    a) With a partner, role play a point-counterpoint discussion on the statement, "Governments should not give grants to make higher education cheaper. Students should pay the full cost of these services themselves. Taxpayers should not contribute to the cost of an individual's higher education."
    b) After the role play, explain to your partner what you really believe and why.

Preparing for a Career as a Social Service Worker

Different levels of government provide various social services to their communities. Have you ever considered a career helping people who are experiencing social problems? Social service workers help people, as individuals or in groups, to deal with difficulties that may be the result of disabilities, discrimination based on gender or race, financial problems, or emotional and mental health problems. Some social service workers are employed by private organizations, and some work for organizations funded or run by government.

Social service workers provide help through counselling, group work, community outreach, or correctional services. They need to be good listeners and able

FIGURE 2–9

Social service workers may help to build a sense of community by bringing together various groups.

to provide support. They need to understand the legal system as it relates to people's rights, and they need to know about resources available to help people deal with a variety of social problems.

Many community colleges offer two-year programs to train social service workers. They are a blend of in-class instruction and field work in a social service agency. The following program is typical.

Social Service Worker College Program

Semester 1

- Urban sociology
- Human growth and behaviour
- Orientation to human services
- Information and referral skills
- Interpersonal skills
- Field practice orientation
- Communications

Semester 2

- Political process
- Interviewing skills 1
- Field practice 1
- Family dynamics
- Integrative seminar 1
- Cross-cultural skills
- Communications
- General education

Semester 3

- Group work skills
- Special needs populations
- Field practice 2
- Integrative seminar 2
- Current social policy issues
- Interviewing skills 2
- Community development

Semester 4

- Agency administration and fundraising
- Legislation in human services
- Field practice 3
- Integrative seminar 3
- Introduction to life skills
- Case management
- General education

Source: Humber College Calendar, 1995.

Activities

16. Look through a listing of courses offered in your school. If you were considering entering a program to train as a social services worker, what high school courses do you think you should take? Why?

17. The following interests and skills are considered necessary for success in a social services worker program. Rate yourself on a scale of 1 (low) to 5 (high) for each one.
    a) Capacity to develop self-awareness, maturity, and initiative
    b) Respect for individual and group differences
    c) Strength under stress and ability to meet deadlines
    d) Good communications skills, both written and oral
    e) Ability to work independently and with others
    f) Ability to deal with situations in a positive way
    Based on the ratings you gave yourself, how well have you already acquired the skills and interests necessary for this type of work?

18. An entry requirement for most social services worker programs is a minimum of 50 hours of documented volunteer experience in a recognized human services organization. Look in the telephone directory for your area. Identify three organizations for which you would consider volunteering, if you were trying to get into the program.

19. How interested would you be in a career as a social services worker? Explain.

Does Our Government Need Reform?

In any healthy society, there is discussion about possible reforms to make government more effective. In this regard, Canada is no exception. Three types of reform, in particular, seem to attract much attention.

Recalling Elected Representatives

Under Canadian election laws, a person elected to represent a riding in either the national or a provincial government may hold that position until the next election. This could be up to five years away. What happens, however, if voters in the riding are not happy with the person's performance as their representative? What happens if, for example, facts come to light about the MP's past that make him or her seem unsuitable as a representative? At present, there is no way for the voters to **recall** — or replace — their representative.

> British Columbia has considered a plan for recalling provincial members of its legislative assembly. These proposals have not been adopted, but would it be a good idea to do so? Would the proposals give voters more control over their representatives? Or would they just encourage discontented people to make mischief?
>
> - A new election would be held in a riding if 50 percent of the voters, plus one, signed a petition to hold one.
>
> - No petition for recall could be presented during the first 18 months of a member's term.
>
> *Source: Report of the British Columbia Committee on Parliamentary Reform, November 1993.*

Choosing Parliament in a Different Way

In each of Canada's ridings, voters choose a person to be their representative in the House of Commons. Look at the results shown in Figure 2–10. The graph shows that, in the 1993 election, Murray Calder won only 36 percent of the votes, but was still chosen as the riding's MP because he won more votes than anyone else. He was **"first past the post" (FPTP)**. Similar voting patterns in other ridings meant that the Liberal Party won 41 percent of the votes cast, but 60 percent of the seats in the House of Commons. The Progressive Conservatives, by contrast, won 16 percent of the votes, but fewer than 1 percent of the seats.

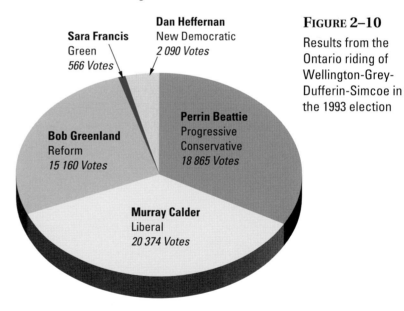

Sara Francis
Green
566 Votes

Dan Heffernan
New Democratic
2 090 Votes

Bob Greenland
Reform
15 160 Votes

Perrin Beattie
Progressive
Conservative
18 865 Votes

Murray Calder
Liberal
20 374 Votes

FIGURE 2–10

Results from the Ontario riding of Wellington-Grey-Dufferin-Simcoe in the 1993 election

Some critics of the Canadian system of voting say that our present method results in parliaments that do not accurately represent what the voters want.

Some countries — for example, Holland and Israel — use a system known as **proportional representation (PR)**. In this system, people vote for lists of candidates rather than for a single representative. If a party gets 41 percent of the votes, it gets 41 percent of the seats in parliament. But that system also has its critics. In 1993, Italy switched away from PR, because too many small parties were winning seats and no party was large enough to maintain power. Whenever the small parties joined together, they could vote the government out.

Some Canadians support **FPTP-PR**, a compromise between the two systems. They feel that an **FPTP-PR** system produces a parliament more in line with what voters as a group want. As yet, though, no major political party has declared its support for it.

FIGURE 2–11

This ballot is from Holland, where a system of PR is used. The ballot has been greatly reduced and only a portion is shown here. Its actual size is 70 cm x 50 cm. Compare this ballot with the one shown in Figure 1–16. What disadvantages do you see with the Dutch ballot?

Germany's FPTP-PR system of voting is a compromise between "first past the post" and proportional representation.

- Voters cast two votes — one for a representative in their riding, and one for the party of their choice.

- Half the members of the German parliament come from the riding votes, and the other half from the party votes.

Table 2–3 Result of Canada's election of 1993 compared with result if FPTP-PR had been used. Would FPTP-PR have made a significant difference to the House of Commons? Explain.

Liberals	B.Q.	Reform	N.D.P.	P.C.	Independent
Actual result					
177	54	52	9	2	1
If FPTP-PR used					
145	40	52	15	35	8

FIGURE 2–12

Two members of a Slavic minority group wear traditional costume to vote in an election in Germany. Representatives of smaller groups are more likely to win seats in parliament in a system of proportional representation.

Reforming the Senate

Some people criticize our present system of choosing representatives because it is entirely based on representation by population. The larger a province's population, the more seats it gets in the House of Commons. Ontario gets 99 seats under this system, and Quebec 75. These provinces have a combined total of almost 59 percent of the seats. In other provinces, particularly British Columbia and Alberta, there is widespread support for trying to balance our "rep by pop" system in the House of Commons with a reformed Senate.

Currently, senators are appointed by the governor general on the advice of the prime minister. They have two main functions. The first is to review bills that have been passed by the House of Commons. Senators have the power to reject bills or suggest changes. In this way, they serve to check the power of the House of Commons. The second function of the Senate is to investigate a variety of important issues, including the concerns of various regions in the country.

One of the most popular proposals for reform is the "**Triple-E Senate**." Supporters of this reform say that Triple-E will give provinces with smaller populations a greater chance of being heard in national politics.

Total 104

FIGURE 2–13

Senate seats by region, 1995

The Triple-E Senate

- In the senate, all provinces would have an EQUAL number of representatives (senators).

- All senators would be ELECTED by their home province.

- The senate would have an EFFECTIVE role, including the right to reject laws passed by the House of Commons.

FIGURE 2–14

The Senate chamber. This photograph shows a special ceremony marking the installation of a new governor general, Romeo LeBlanc.

FIGURE 2–15

This cartoon gives one extreme view of Senate reform. What does it suggest?

Activities

20. a) Under what circumstances might voters wish to recall their MP?

    b) According to the British Columbia proposals, under what circumstances could a new election be held in a riding, if voters were dissatisfied with their representative?

21. a) Under the FPTP-PR system, how do voters vote?

    b) Make a bar graph based on the information in Table 2–3. Show the seats won by each party in 1993 and the seats they would have won if FPTP-PR had been in effect. Which parties would have won more seats under FPTP-PR? Which parties would have lost seats? Which parties would have remained the same? What other conclusions can you draw from your graph?

    c) Do you think that FPTP-PR is a better or worse system than the one we now use? Explain your reasons.

22. a) What is the meaning of "rep by pop"?

    b) What do the critics of rep by pop say about its effect on government in Canada?

    c) How would a Triple-E Senate balance the effect of rep by pop?

    d) Do you think that a Triple-E Senate would be a worthwhile reform? Why or why not?

23. Imagine you had the power to introduce the three changes outlined in this section: Recalling MPs, FPTP-PR voting, and a Triple-E Senate. In what order would you place them, from most important to least important? Explain your reasoning.

24. With the help of your teacher, hold formal debates in class about the following statements.

    a) The Triple-E Senate would make our political system more fair.

    b) Voters in all ridings should have the power, two years after an election, to recall their MP, if they feel that he or she is not doing a good job of representing them.

    c) FPTP-PR is a better system for choosing governments than the present First Past the Post system.

25. Use a source with detailed statistics about Canada to do the following activities. Suitable sources include almanacs, atlases, and the Canada Yearbook. Your librarian might also be able to suggest sources on CD-ROM.

    a) Find out the total population of each of the seven regions identified in Figure 2–13.

    b) Find out the value of the Gross Domestic Product (GDP) generated in each of the seven regions. (GDP is the value of all goods and services produced in one year. Provincial GDPs are sometimes referred to as Gross Provincial Product.)

c) Based on these figures, does it appear that the regions are properly represented in the Senate?

26. Imagine that the government is considering reforming the Senate on a geographic system of regional representation. The following geographic regions have been identified:

- Atlantic   - Great Lakes-St. Lawrence
- Near North   - Prairies
- Far North   - Western Mountains

Work in small groups (six in total). Each group should examine a different geographic region.

a) Calculate the approximate population of your group's region. You may have to make some educated guesses, and negotiate with other groups. For example, Manitoba is divided between the Prairies, Near North, and Far North regions, but most of the major towns and cities are in the Prairies region. The three regional groups might agree to assign 70 percent of Manitoba's population to Prairies, 28 percent to Near North, and 2 percent to Far North.

b) Calculate the approximate Gross Domestic Product of your group's region, using the same procedure as above.

c) Identify the main characteristics of each region. Consider factors of climate, landforms, transportation, and economic activity.

d) Collect the findings from each region.
Either
  i) Prepare a report for the purposes of Senate reform. Would a system of representation based on geographic regions be better than the present one based on population regions? Would it be better than one based on economic production? What are the reasons for your conclusions?

or

  ii) Hold a debate in which you role play representatives of the region your group has studied. Using the information you have gathered, argue for or against reform of the Senate based on geographic regions.

PUTTING IT TOGETHER

1 a) Find out the following information about the three levels of government as they affect you. Make sure that you find out information for national, provincial, and local levels. There will probably be three answers to each of the questions.
  i) Where is it situated?
  ii) What is the name of the representative for your riding?
  iii) What are some of its major responsibilities?
  iv) How does it raise money from the people?
  v) What are some of its important achievements in your area?

b) Create your own organizer to record the information you have collected. Incorporate some pictures or drawings to illustrate some of your information.

c) Based on your findings, which level of government seems to have the greatest impact on your part of Canada? Why is this so?

2 Make an organizer similar to the one below, and complete it with information from this chapter. Follow the example.

Key terms relating to Canada's government		
Term	**Meaning**	**Purpose**
Cabinet	Prime minister and advisors chosen from MPs	Suggests bills to parliament that may become laws
Representation by population		
Levels of government		
Executive		
Legislative		
Judicial		
Recall		
FPTP-PR		
Triple-E Senate		

PART 3

THE JUDICIAL SYSTEM

*T*he English word **judicial** means "relating to a court or legal case." The judicial system refers to the various courts, judges, lawyers, and others responsible for dealing with legal cases. Let us look at an example of a particular case.

Suppose a Level 1 learner driver was pulled over by police, shortly after midnight, on an expressway, with no one else in the car. Such a driver would be charged with three separate violations of the licence law. (Check the description below to see if you can identify the three violations.) Now it must be decided if the accused person is guilty. It is not the police who decide — they only charge the individual. It is up to the courts — the judicial system — to decide.

Time Line of a Court Case

Level 1 driver charged with offences.	February 17
First meeting with lawyer to discuss case.	February 20
Meeting with lawyer to discuss police evidence.	March 24
At meeting with lawyer, accused decides to plead guilty.	May 5
Accused pleads guilty in court. Judge fines accused $200, suspends licence for 12 months.	June 27
Driver re-applies for Level 1 licence.	June 28 (following year)

The Graduated Driver's Licence System

Successfully developed in New Zealand in the early 1990s, the graduated driver's licence system has been copied in various forms in a number of provinces in Canada. The graduated system places limits on all new drivers, regardless of their age.

The following examples are taken from the Ontario system, introduced in 1994.

Level 1 (Valid 5 Years) *

Drivers remain in this category for a minimum of 12 months. They must have a licensed driver with at least 4 years' experience with them in the front of the car. They are not permitted any alcohol at all in their bloodstream, and they may not drive between midnight and 5 a.m. or on expressways.

After 12 months, drivers may take a road test to obtain a Level 2 licence.

Level 2 (Valid 12 Months)

Drivers may drive unaccompanied at any time of day or night. Passengers are limited to the number of seatbelts available. Drivers are not permitted any alcohol at all in their bloodstream. After 12 months, Level Two licence holders may apply for a full licence.

* Level 1 may be shortened by four months if the driver has successfully completed an approved driver-training program.

YOUNG DRIVERS OF CANADA

FIGURE 3-1

Imagine you are a lawyer opposed to what you see as increasing government restrictions on individual freedom. What arguments would you use in court to attack the Graduated Licence System? What arguments would the prosecution make in favour of the system?

FIGURE 3-2

What reasons can you think of to explain why younger drivers tend to have a higher than average collision rate? Do you think the graduated licence system would help to reduce the collision rate? What steps can young drivers take to help ensure safety on the road?

Key Words

- criminal law
- civil law
- testimony
- summary offence
- indictable offence
- magistrate
- preliminary hearing
- trial by judge
- trial by judge and jury
- Legal Aid
- Crown attorney
- cross-examine
- damages
- plaintiff
- Writ of Summons
- defendant
- Examination for Discovery
- rehabilitation
- retribution
- young offender
- deterrent

Looking Forward

- How does the court system work?

- What is the difference between a criminal and a civil case?

- How should we deal with people who break the law?

- Should the Young Offenders Act be reformed?

How the Court System Works

The largest number of cases before courts involve **criminal law**. In these cases, people have been charged with offences that are against the law. Crimes are divided into a number of categories, however, depending on their severity (see Table 3–1). The courts may use various methods to try people accused of crimes (see Table 3–2). In addition, there are a number of different courts to deal with different types of cases (see Figure 3–4). Some of these courts hear cases in **civil law**—that is, private disputes between parties.

Summary offences are those for which the maximum penalty is less than two years' imprisonment.

Indictable offences (pronounced *in-DITE-able*) are those for which the maximum penalty is two years or more.

Table 3–1 Categories of crime in Canada

Category	Examples	Typical penalties
a) Summary offences	Common assault Trespassing Disorderly conduct	Probation Fine Volunteer work 2 years less a day in prison
b) Indictable offences i) Less serious	Theft under $1000 Assault causing bodily harm	Probation Fine Volunteer work 2-5 years in prison
ii) Serious	Drug trafficking Armed robbery Manslaughter	Fine 5-10 years in prison
iii) Most serious	Kidnapping Murder	10 years to life in prison

Table 3–2 How criminal cases are tried (Adult Court)

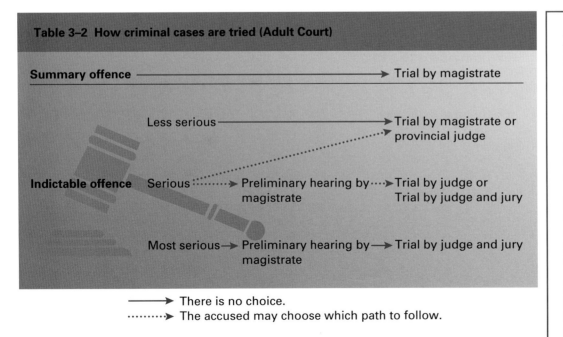

Summary offence ——————————————→ Trial by magistrate

Indictable offence

Less serious ——————————————→ Trial by magistrate or provincial judge

Serious ·····→ Preliminary hearing by magistrate ····→ Trial by judge or Trial by judge and jury

Most serious → Preliminary hearing by magistrate → Trial by judge and jury

——→ There is no choice.
········→ The accused may choose which path to follow.

A **magistrate** is a person with legal training who may be in charge of preliminary hearings and minor court cases.

A **preliminary hearing** is held in a court to decide whether there is enough evidence against the accused to hold a full-scale trial.

In **trial by judge**, the judge decides whether or not the accused is guilty, and sentences the accused if found guilty.

In **trial by judge and jury**, the jury decides whether or not the accused is guilty, and the judge sentences the accused if necessary.

FIGURE 3–3

The jury decides whether or not the accused is guilty. Do some research into how a jury is selected. What is the role of the foreperson? Why would it be important that the jury represent the gender, cultural, and occupational make-up of the community as a whole?

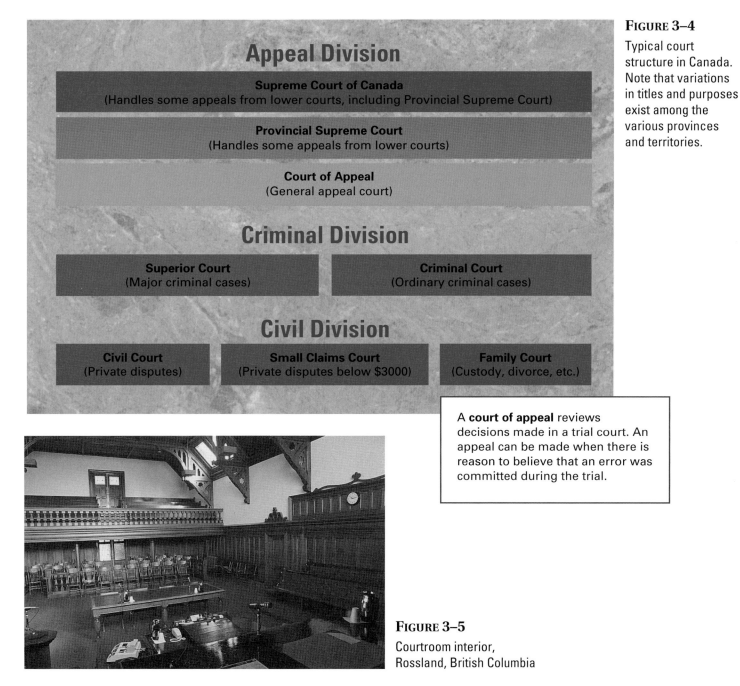

FIGURE 3–4

Typical court structure in Canada. Note that variations in titles and purposes exist among the various provinces and territories.

Appeal Division

Supreme Court of Canada
(Handles some appeals from lower courts, including Provincial Supreme Court)

Provincial Supreme Court
(Handles some appeals from lower courts)

Court of Appeal
(General appeal court)

Criminal Division

Superior Court
(Major criminal cases)

Criminal Court
(Ordinary criminal cases)

Civil Division

Civil Court
(Private disputes)

Small Claims Court
(Private disputes below $3000)

Family Court
(Custody, divorce, etc.)

A **court of appeal** reviews decisions made in a trial court. An appeal can be made when there is reason to believe that an error was committed during the trial.

FIGURE 3–5

Courtroom interior, Rossland, British Columbia

1. For each of the following terms write a definition and an example:
   a) a summary offence
   b) an indictable offence
   c) a most serious indictable offence

2. For each of the following terms, write a definition in your own words:
   a) a magistrate
   b) a preliminary hearing
   c) trial by judge
   d) trial by judge and jury

3. a) Look at Table 3–1. What evidence is there to suggest that as crimes become more serious, so do the penalties that go with them?
   b) What reasons can you suggest to explain why this is so?

4. a) Look at Table 3–2. What evidence is there to suggest that as crimes become more serious, there is a greater attempt to give accused people a chance to prove their innocence?
   b) What reasons can you think of to suggest why this is so?

A Civil and a Criminal Case

On February 17, Alan Fields and Rosemary Tan entered a bank at Main and Spruce Streets. They pulled out handguns, held up the tellers, and robbed them of $1700. Rushing out of the bank to get away, Rosemary Tan collided with a pedestrian, Gladys McCarthy, knocking her to the ground. Mrs. McCarthy chipped two natural teeth as she hit the ground, and her dentures were broken. She later faced dental bills of over $2000 to repair the damage.

The robbery had been recorded on the bank's video surveillance system. Although the pictures were blurred and grainy, a positive identification was made and Fields and Tan were arrested that afternoon.

Fields and Tan faced charges related to the bank robbery in criminal court. They also had a civil court case related to the accident they had with Gladys McCarthy.

FIGURE 3–6
Fields and Tan consult with their lawyer at the police station after their arrest.

FIGURE 3–7
Fields and Tan enter their plea in court.

The Criminal Case: A Time Line

FIGURE 3–8
The Crown attorney makes his opening statement to the jury.

February 17

- Alan Fields and Rosemary Tan were charged with (a) armed robbery and (b) pointing a firearm in a threatening way.
- Fields and Tan consulted a lawyer at the police station. Because they could not afford a lawyer, one was provided by **Legal Aid**, a fund to provide free legal advice.

February 18

- Fields and Tan were formally charged with the crimes in court.
- Their lawyer requested that they be released on **bail** (allowed to remain free until trial, after paying a sum of money as a security to ensure return for trail).
- Magistrate refused. Fields and Tan held in jail.

June 4

- Fields and Tan appeared at preliminary hearing before magistrate.
- **Crown attorney** (lawyer for prosecution) called tellers and customers in bank as witnesses.

Answering Crown attorney's questions, they said what they had seen.
- Defence lawyer **cross-examined** witnesses (asked them questions to challenge their evidence).
- Defence lawyer could, but chose not to, present evidence for the accused.
- Magistrate ruled that there was a case to answer, and ordered Fields and Tan to stand trial. They chose to be tried by judge and jury.
- Defence lawyer applied for bail. Refused.

September 7-10

- Trial began before judge and jury of 12 people.
- Charges read out. Accused pleaded "not guilty."
- Crown attorney and defence lawyer made opening statements to jury about what they would try to show.

- Crown attorney called witnesses who appeared at preliminary hearing. They answered questions, as they did at preliminary hearing. Two additional witnesses were called. They answered questions. Crown attorney showed surveillance video. Defence lawyer cross-examined witnesses, trying to challenge their ability to recognize the accused as the robbers. Defence lawyer also challenged clarity of video evidence.
- Defence lawyer separately called Fields and Tan. Under questioning they claimed an **alibi** (that they were somewhere else at the time of the crime). They claimed to have been shopping on the other side of town. Defence lawyer also called a friend of the accused who claimed to have been

with them at the time of the crime.
- Crown attorney cross-examined witnesses to challenge their reliability, accusing them of **perjury** (lying in court).
- Defence lawyer addressed jury to outline main points of the case. Asked jury to find the accused not guilty.
- Crown attorney addressed the jury. Asked them to find the accused guilty.
- Judge reviewed the main points of the case as presented by Crown attorney and defence lawyer. Judge advised jury how much evidence was needed to find the accused guilty. Judge explained that if the jury was not sure, it had to find the accused not guilty.
- Jury went to jury room to discuss case. All twelve members had to agree that accused were guilty before they could convict Fields and Tan.
- Jury returned to court. Foreperson announced that accused were guilty.
- Judge sentenced accused to 7 years' imprisonment, starting from February 17. (Accused had been in jail since then, awaiting trial.)

FIGURE 3–9
The jury foreperson reads the verdict.

The Civil Case: A Time Line

February 20

- Mrs. McCarthy hired a lawyer to recover **damages** (money to pay for a wrong) from Fields and Tan, to pay for her dental bills. Lawyer advised her to wait until criminal trial was complete. If accused were found guilty, damages might be easier to get.

October 15

- Mrs. McCarthy was the **plaintiff** (the person claiming a wrong). The plaintiff's lawyer obtained a **Writ of Summons** from civil court. This is a document outlining the details of the plaintiff's case in claiming damages. If **defendants** (the people from whom damages are being claimed) do not respond to the writ, they automatically lose the case.

November 27

- Defendants' lawyer appeared in court to request an **Examination for Discovery** (a hearing held in a Special Examiner's office where lawyers could question each other's witnesses).
- Examination set for December 14. Hearing set for March 13.

December 14

- At Examination for Discovery, the two lawyers questioned witnesses for the other side, to find out the basis of their case.

March 13

- Hearing opened before a judge.
- Lawyers for plaintiff and defendants made opening statements to judge.
- Plaintiff's lawyer called witnesses. Defendants' lawyer cross-examined them.
- Defendants' lawyer called witnesses. Plaintiff's lawyer cross-examined them.

- Lawyers for defendants and plaintiff made closing statements to judge.
- Judge found for (agreed with) plaintiff. Ordered the defendants to pay her $2500 for dental bills, plus $1000 for pain and suffering.

FIGURE 3–10

The Examination for Discovery

FIGURE 3–11

Mrs. McCarthy giving evidence in the court. Is she the plaintiff or the defendant in this case? What is the difference?

Activities

5. Make an organizer similar to the one below, but make sure that you place the various stages of a criminal case **in the correct order**. Complete the right-hand column of the organizer.

Stages of a Criminal Case

Stages	What happens
Jury considers case in the jury room	Reviews evidence. Decides whether accused are guilty or not.
Accused plead guilty or not guilty	
Judge sentences accused	
Accused charged by police	
Judge reviews evidence and instructs jury	
Preliminary hearing	
Defence lawyer calls witnesses; Crown attorney cross-examines	
Both sides make closing statements to jury	
Jury pronounces accused guilty	
Both sides make closing statements to jury	
Crown attorney calls witnesses; Defence lawyer cross examines	

6. Make an organizer similar to the one below, but make sure that you place the various stages of a civil case **in the correct order**. Complete the right-hand column of the organizer.

Stages of a Civil Case

Stages	What happens
Defendants' lawyer requests Examination for Discovery	Wants to question plaintiff's lawyer's witnesses
Defendants' lawyer calls witnesses; Plaintiff's lawyer cross-examines	
Examination for Discovery held before Special Examiner	
Lawyers make opening statements to judge; Plaintiff's lawyer goes first	
Plaintiff's lawyer calls witnesses; Defendants' lawyer cross-examines	
Plaintiff's lawyer issues Writ of Summons	
Case sent from Examination for Discovery to hearing before judge	

7. a) Identify five ways in which procedures in criminal and civil cases are the same.

   b) Identify five ways in which procedures in criminal and civil cases are different.

   c) Which do you think are more significant, the similarities or the differences? Explain.

8. Form two groups. One group should be two-thirds of the class (criminal case group), the other group should be the remaining one-third (civil case group). Re-enact all the stages of the Fields and Tan criminal and civil court cases, using the time lines of the cases as a guide.

How Should We Deal with Lawbreakers?

Canadians are divided about the best way to deal with people convicted of breaking the law, especially those convicted of serious crimes. Should we try to educate them about the error of their ways (**rehabilitation**)? Or should we punish them severely for their actions (**retribution**)? Consider the following cases.

> Everyone has the right not to be subjected to cruel and unusual treatment or punishment.
>
> *Canadian Charter of Rights and Freedoms, Section 12*

FIGURE 3–13

A prison sentence is the most common form of retribution in Canada. What is the purpose of sending criminals to prison?

FIGURE 3–12

Rehabilitation program in prison. How will the skills being learned here benefit both the inmates and society?

Unspeakable Crimes

ON ONE side of the packed courtroom sat the grief-stricken parents of the two young murder victims. Near the opposite wall sat the family of the accused. Between them, an attractive 23-year-old woman named Karla Homolka gazed impassively…as Crown Attorney Murray Segal stepped up to the lectern in the St. Catharines, Ont., courtroom. For the next 27 minutes, Segal read a statement outlining in stark and shocking detail the role that Homolka played in the deaths of teenagers Leslie Mahaffy and Kristen French. While others in the room gasped and wept, the elegantly dressed Homolka dabbed her eyes with a handkerchief — a rare display of public emotion by a woman at the centre of one of Canada's most horrific criminal cases. But Segal's tersely worded statement could not begin to explain how a young woman from a stable middle-class family could commit such unspeakable acts.

Leslie Mahaffy, at the time of her death a 14-year-old Grade 9 student in Burlington, Ont., was last seen by friends in the early morning of June 15, 1991. Two weeks later — on the day that Homolka married Paul Bernardo, a 26-year-old trainee accountant — parts of Mahaffy's body were found encased in concrete in Lake Gibson, a reservoir just south of St. Catharines. Ten months later, on April 16, 1992, Kristen French, a 15-year-old St. Catharines high-school student was abducted while walking home from school. Her nude body was found two weeks later on a county road near Burlington. Police maintain that both girls were sexually assaulted….

During a 75-minute address, [Judge Kovacs] explains that Homolka was charged with manslaughter because she bears responsibility for the deaths of Leslie Mahaffy and Kristen French even though she did not personally kill them…. [She alleged that her husband, Paul Bernardo, had done that.] Homolka has committed the worst offence he explains, but she is not the worst conceivable offender. She has co-operated fully with the police…. She has also spared everyone the expense and trauma of a long trial….

Source: Maclean's *magazine, July 19, 1993, p. 14.*

FIGURE 3–14

David Milgaard (left), shown here together with Donald Marshall, who was also imprisoned (for 11 years) for a crime he did not commit. Although a Royal Commission of Inquiry concluded that Marshall, a member of the Micmac First Nation, had suffered from a "two-tier system of justice" in which Aboriginal people were not given the same consideration as others, Marshall himself did not appear to be bitter. "It's not just me; it's the next guy that comes along," he told reporters on his release. Should the cases of Milgaard and Marshall have any bearing on the way we deal with people convicted of crimes? Why or why not?

23 Years in Prison for a Crime He Didn't Commit

DAVID MILGAARD was sentenced to prison in 1969 for the murder of Gail Miller, in Saskatoon, Saskatchewan. Being convicted of first-degree murder, he received a sentence of life imprisonment, meaning that he must serve a minimum of 25 years before being released. There was only one problem. He was not guilty. The trial he received was not entirely fair. Evidence favourable to his defence was hidden. In 1992, the Supreme Court of Canada ordered his immediate release. This is what he had to say about the law.

On prisons: It is insane to place a man in a box or a cage for 25 years…. There is no caring in these places. Look at what happens to women inside prison. It is ludicrous to have people sit inside prisons and do nothing with their lives. There is a better way to handle people…. The worst time I had in prison was when my grandmother died and I was not able to get out to be at the funeral….

On the justice system: The justice system failed us miserably…. I am bitter against the system. I love people. The Canadian criminal system is there to protect people. A perfect justice system would be mercifully [fair], not punishment-oriented….

On his demand for compensation: …Saskatchewan says that it will block compensation. I am going to have to go on welfare. I came out of prison with about $240. After 23 years, that is all I have. Except for my parents, I am out on the street.

Source: Maclean's *magazine, April 27, 1992, pp. 44–45.*

Activities

9. a) How far do you think Judge Kovacs should have used the principles of rehabilitation in sentencing Karla Homolka for her crimes?

   b) How far should he have used the principles of retribution?

   c) Homolka was sentenced to two **concurrent prison terms** (running at the same time), each of 12 years. If she had part of her sentence **remitted** (suspended), because she showed evidence of reform and regret for her crimes, she could be released from prison in as few as 4 years. Do you think that she was properly sentenced? Explain your reasons.

10. a) Do you agree with any of David Milgaard's remarks? Do you disagree with any? Give reasons for your views.

    b) If you had the power, what would you do for David Milgaard or Donald Marshall, to try to compensate for the years wrongly spent in prison?

11. TV cameras are regularly allowed in American courtrooms, but excluded from Canadian ones.

    a) With a partner role play a point-counter-point discussion on the statement, "TV cameras should not be allowed in Canadian courtrooms."

    b) After the role play, explain to your partner what you really believe and why.

Should We Reform the *Young Offenders Act?*

In Canada, any person aged at least 12 but not yet 18 who commits a crime is considered a **young offender**. For such a person, the law grants special protections.

In Britain, in 1993, two 11-year-old boys were sentenced to life imprisonment for the murder of a 3-year-old. They would have to serve a minimum of 15 years before release. The case sparked a debate in Canada about our *Young Offenders Act*. In Canada, the boys would not have been charged with a crime, for they were under 12 years of age.

There is a wide range of opinions in Canada on the *Young Offenders Act*. Consider the information on these two pages and try to form your own opinions.

Special Legal Protections Granted to Young Offenders

- Media may not identify by name, picture, or description any young offender.

- The court must give greater weight to reforming (not punishing) the young offender than it would if the offender were an adult.

- Maximum penalty for any offence for someone tried as a young offender, is 5 years' imprisonment (raised from 3 years in 1992).

- In exceptional cases, where a judge agrees to try a 16- or 17-year-old in adult court for a most serious crime, maximum penalty is 10 years' imprisonment.

Two Canadian Cases

In 1992, David Andrew Fraser, who was then 15, fatally stabbed 13-year-old Ryan Garrioch with a 22-cm kitchen knife, in a Calgary schoolyard. In court, David admitted planning the attack all weekend; it took place on a Monday. He also admitted to having a problem with controlling anger. He was tried in adult court and sentenced to the maximum 10-year sentence.

In Regina, in 1992, parents were angry that no one would be charged in the alleged abduction and sexual assault of two boys aged 8 and 9. Apparently, the boys were abducted, chained to a pipe on an office-building roof, and sexually assaulted. The two boys who were allegedly responsible for the crime were 8 and 11 years old, and could not therefore be charged with an offence.

Some Facts About Young Offender Crime

- Only 13 percent of charges against young offenders involve violence.

- The murder rate — a good indicator of violent crime levels — remained the same for young offenders from 1986 to 1991.

- Over 65 percent of convictions against young offenders are for property crimes such as theft.

Based on report by the Justice Department, Ottawa, 1993.

Transfer to Adult Court

If a young person is charged with a serious offence such as murder, the case may be transferred to adult court. The judge will consider the age of the young person's needs, and the needs of society before ordering the transfer. Once the young person is in adult court, he or she will no longer be protected by the special conditions that apply to young offenders.

FIGURE 3–15

These materials were produced by ProAction, a coalition of concerned citizens and police in Toronto. ProAction sponsors events that help young people and police officers get to know and trust each other. What is its message about crime and young offenders? Do you think this is an effective way to deal with crime by young people?

"We can fight youth crime with guns, handcuffs and longer jail terms."

"Or we can use baseballs, hockey pucks and minnows."

We can fight youth crime by pursuing and punishing the guilty. That's a vital part of what Metro's police force does.

But what we can also do is get to innocent kids before their young lives take a tragic turn to crime. Before they get caught up in a cycle that ruins individuals and destroys families.

And that's the purpose behind ProAction. ProAction is a Toronto citizens foundation whose purpose is to bridge the gap between cops and kids in our community. To get to know each other one on one. To give kids someone to turn to. To see our cops as human beings instead of uniforms.

ProAction funds sports programs, day trips and community events that help cops and kids get to know each other and create a common bond.

And it's not just a good idea that could work. It already is working.

Cops and kids and baseballs.

To date, our projects have involved more than 500 Metro police officers and have reached more than 15,000 kids. Our cops took part in a wide variety of programs all across the city.

We helped fund a multi-cultural baseball tournament in East Agincourt. We pitched in when the St. Rose-St. Thomas softball league needed some new equipment. And baseball wasn't the only sport for cops and kids to get together. We gave money for cops to help out the West End Basketball League at Jane & Woolner and the youth league in the Humber Boulevard area. We helped cops shoot hoops with kids in the Flemingdon Park Youth Program basketball tournament. And we helped purchase uniforms for two girls basketball teams in the Toronto Lithuanian AUSRA Sports Clubs.

In addition, we helped our cops get involved in cricket teams, volleyball tourneys, hockey leagues, skiing and even horseback riding.

Kids and cops and sports. We helped them get together for a little healthy competition.

Cops and kids and the great outdoors.

We also got involved in events taking Metro police and youth outside of the city.

We helped get them out of town on a day trip to Gananoque. We helped some cops and kids catch some rays at Wasaga Beach. We funded a field trip to Kelso Conservation Area as part of the Chinese and Vietnamese Youth Outreach Project of the Scadding Court Community Centre.

And we helped pitch a few tents on a camping weekend for kids and cops from the Jane-Finch and Malvern area. We even helped some cops take kids ice-fishing up on Lake Simcoe for a day. The way we figure it, if we can take kids outside the normal environment, they can get to know our cops a little better.

Cops and kids and get-togethers.

We helped cops and kids get to know each other better at a number of community events held across the city.

Some Opinions About Young Offender Crime

"We've got kids here younger than 12 committing criminal acts and they understand what they are doing."

Head of Youth Crime Division, Winnipeg Police

"[If you reduce the minimum age] where do you stop? Do you charge 7-year-olds? It's a real dilemma."

President, Manitoba Defence Lawyers' Association

"Maybe the *Young Offenders Act* was a step too far forward. The question is, do we want to step as far back as the British?"

Lawyer specializing in youth crimes

"A 10- or 11-year-old can commit murder and literally get away with it…. It's time to stop treating 17-year-olds like babies. If we prosecute them in adult court, it would act as a **deterrent** [it would discourage crime] to criminal behaviour for themselves and their peers."

Member of parliament

"Youth crime is not skyrocketing as many people believe, but is at about the same level as five or ten years ago…. This may surprise some people…. Canadians are more concerned about youth crime now than they have been at times in the past."

Report by the Justice Department, Ottawa, 1993

Activities

12. Summarize, in your own words, the special legal protections granted to young offenders.

13. Read over the different quotations and pieces of information in this section.
    a) Classify them into two groups — those generally supportive of the present *Young Offenders Act* and those critical of it.
    b) With which group do you generally agree? Why?

14. For each of the following possible changes to the *Young Offenders Act*, write an imaginary letter to the editor of a national newspaper, stating whether you agree or disagree. Remember that letters to the editor are samples of persuasive writing. They must contain powerful language, a strong sense of your audience, and a clear statement of what action is necessary.
    a) Lower the age at which a person could be charged with an offence to 10.
    b) Lower the age at which a person would become liable to trial as an adult to 16.
    c) Try all young offenders as adults if they commit most serious crimes such as murder or sexual assault.
    d) Make it legal to publish the identity of young offenders convicted of crimes.
    e) Give greater weight to punishing — not reforming — convicted young offenders, in an attempt to discourage others from committing crimes.

15. a) Do some research into the rates of recidivism — the percentage of people who return to prison after committing further offences. Research also the way in which inmates are treated in Canadian prisons.
    b) Hold a class debate on the statement, "The recidivism rate shows that current prison practices do not work, and that changes need to be made."

PUTTING IT TOGETHER

1 a) Rank the following legal occupations from 1 (most challenging and interesting) to 7 (least challenging and interesting) from your point of view.
    magistrate
    defence lawyer
    police officer
    Crown attorney
    plaintiff's lawyer (civil case)
    Special Examiner
    judge
   b) Explain the reasons for your rankings.

2 Look through newspapers and magazines. Cut out stories that refer to current Canadian legal cases. Make a collage of the cases, showing for each one:

   a) whether it is civil or criminal.
   b) the accused/defendant.
   c) the plaintiff.
   d) who will decide on the outcome of the case.
   e) what are the major facts in the case.
   f) which side you think should win, and why.

Include visuals where you can.